GREETINGS FROM THE UNITED KINGDOM

ONE DAY, THE KID GOAT WAS PLAYING ON THE GRASS IN HER NEIGHBOURHOOD. HER PARENTS GONE TO WORK...

...WHEN SUDDENLY, A KID LION APPEARED FROM NOWHERE AND JOINED HER AT PLAY. HER MOTHER TOO HAS GONE OUT TO WORK.

THEIR FRIENDSHIP BLOSSOMED. THEY ARE SEEN TOGETHER EVERYWHERE AND HAVE BECOME ALMOST INSEPERABLE.

THEN ONE DAY, THE KID LION INVITED HIS FRIEND HOME KNOWING THAT HIS MUM WON'T BE BACK FROM WORK YET.

Lion's Home

THANKS FOR THE GIFTS...GOSH, I SHOULD BE GOING HOME NOW.
THEY PLAYED AS MUCH AS THEY LIKE
WITH LOTS OF GIFTS FOR KID GOAT.
SUDDENLY, KID GOAT REMEMBERS THA
HER MUM WOULD HAVE COME BACK...
OKAY, MY FRIEND. I'L WALK YOU DOWN THE ROAD.
THE KID LION SEES HER OFF AND WAVED HER GOODBYE...
BYE-BYE MY FRIEND SEE YOU SOON.
SEE YOU AND THANKS ONCE AGAIN.
MUM WAS ALREADY AT HOME...LOOKING SAD AND WORRIED.
I'VE BEEN BACK HOME, SINCE HALF HOUR AGC WAITING FOR YOU KID.
SORRY MUM, I HAVE A NEW FRIEND. HE LIVES AT THE **DEN**. HE GAV ME THESE PRESENTS...

OH! THAT'S VERY GENEROUS OF...WHAT! DID YOU SAY DEN?!... THAT'S WHERE THE LIONS LIVE... DON'T YOU EVER GO THERE AGAIN, IT'S VERY DANGEROUS. Y'SEE, THEY KILL US FOR FOOD. WHEN NEXT YOU SEE HIM, DON'T LOOK BACK. JUST RUN FOR YOUR DEAR LIFE, OKAY?
OKAY MUM.
AT THE OTHER SIDE, MOTHER LION WAS WAITING FOR HER SON...ANXIOUSLY
HOPE HE HASN'T FALLEN PREY TO SOME HUNTER
BUT KID LION ARRIVES
WHERE ARE YOU COMING FROM BOY? I'VE BEEN WAITING AND WORRIED FOR YOUR SAFETY.
I'VE JUST SEEN MY NEW FRIEND OFF MUM SHE LIVES IN A PLACE CALLED GRASSLAND.
GRASS-LAND! THAT'S WHERE GOATS LIVE! HA-HA-HA!
...NEXT TIME YOU SEE HER, TEAR HER TO PIECES. SHE'S YOUR FOOD!

THE FISHING EXPEDITION

FREDO LIVES IN KETU TOWN. HE WAS NOT A GOOD HUNTER NOR A GREAT FISHERMAN BUT HE WAS KNOWN FOR HIS TRICKS.

HE LOVES TO OUTSMART PEOPLE. ONE DAY, FREDO CALLED ONE OF HIS FRIENDS

HEY MERO, WHY DON'T WE GO SET TRAPS FOR FISHES. THEN WE'LL SELL THEM AND BECOME QUITE RICH?

WHY NOT FREDO, IT'LL BE FUN TO GO FISHING WITH YOU. WE'LL BECOME RICH...

I'LL BEAT YOU AT YOUR OWN GAME FREDO!

NO FREDO I KNOW YOU. I'M RICH ENOUGH, SO GO AND LOOK FOR ANOTHER VICTIM.

DON'T WORRY, I'LL GET SOMEONE WHO ISN'T SO SMART.

THEN FREDO SAW DADA AND PROPOSED TO HIM. HE AGREED IMMEDIATELY.

1

KOKO AIMED HIS GUN AT THE FATTEST SQUIRREL AND FIRED

BLAM!

VERY SOON THEY CAME TO WHERE THE SQUIRRELS WERE EATING PALM KERNELS AND STOPPED

...A LITTLE TO YOUR RIGHT

YEAH! GOT IT!

KAKA PICKED UP THE DEAD SQUIRREL, VERY HAPPY AND THEY BOTH HEADED BACK HOME TO COOK THEIR MEAL.

AT HOME THEY DEBATED ON HOW TO COOK THE SQUIRREL SOUP.

IT'S OKAY WITH ME KAKA AND THE EARLIER WE START THE BETTER. I'M DYING OF HUNGER ALREADY

KOKO, YOU'LL COOK AND I'LL TELL YOU HOW AND WHEN TO ADD THE CONDIMENTS OKAY?

3

PRIDE GOES BEFORE A FALL

THERE WAS AN UGLY BIRD NAMED TIN-TIN

Tin-Tin was given a special invitation to the birthday party of another bird as the master of ceremony. He knew they wanted to laugh at his looks and voice.

WHY WOULD THEY INVITE ME IF NOT TO MAKE JEST OF ME? AH, THIS IS UNFAIR.

INVITATION

HOW CAN I BE FREE IN A PLACE WHERE THE PEACOCK, THE PARROT, THE NIGHTINGALE AND OTHERS ARE ALL GATHERED TOGETHER?

1

AT THE PARTY, TIN-TIN IMMEDIATELY BECAME THE APPLE OF EVERY EYE. THE SUCCESS WAS SO MUCH FOR HER TO HANDLE AND THE END RESULT WAS PRIDE.
ISN'T SHE BEAUTIFUL?
SHE LOOKS SO GORGEOUS
OH, YOU LOOK SO LOVELY TIN-TIN
OF COURSE I'M THE MOST BEAUTIFUL... MORE BEAUTIFUL THAN YOU ALL PUT TOGETHER, IF YOU DOUBT IT...
...THEN I CHALLENGE ANY OF YOU TO A BEAUTY CONTEST.
?!
!
?
!?
!
?
THEN THE PEACOCK ANSWERED ANGRILY
"HE WHOSE PALM KERNEL WAS CRACKED BY A BENE-VOLENT CIRCUMSTANCE SHOULD NOT FORGET TO BE HUMBLE"... TIN-TIN

TAKING THEIR GAMES WEAPONS AND OTHER NECESSARY ITEMS.
THANK GOD I OILED MY GUN JUST TWO DAYS AGO.
YEAH, AND MINE IS FULLY LOADED... I'M READY IF YOU ARE.
AND THEY SET OFF FOR THE EXPLOIT IN AFRICAN SAFARI
I'M RIGHT BEHIND YOU BUDDY.
AFTER A SHORT WHILE THEY SAW A CLEARANCE
LET'S CAMP HERE SAM.
SURE LIONEL, WHY NOT
AND THEY STARTED BUILDING.
I HOPE THIS ROPE IS TIGHT ENOUGH.
LET ME JOIN THIS TO THAT ONE.

THEY BUILT A SMALL HUT...
...THEIR TEMPORARY HOME AND SLEPT...
AND EARLY THE NEXT MORNING.
LET'S GO AND SHOOT SOME AFRICAN LIONS FOR BREAKFAST SAMSON!
ER...YES, EM.. I MEAN NO, I...I...I'M NOT YET ER... READY...
SAMSON REFUSED TO FOLLOW HIM AFTER MANY ATTEMPTS...
THEN LIONEL DECIDED
I'LL GO AND KILL TWO LIONS...ONE FOR HIM, AND ONE FOR ME.
BUT LIONEL HAD NOT WALKED FAR INTO THE JUNGLE BEFORE HE MET A LION.
ROAAAR!
THE LION LOOKED STRAIGHT AT HIM. LIONEL FELT SO FRIGHTENED THAT HE DROPPED HIS GUN...

HE TURNED ROUND AND RAN FOR DEAR LIFE, BUT THE LION FOLLOWED HIM. HE COULD HEAR ITS FOOTSTEPS CLOSE BY. LIONEL RAN FAST TOWARDS THE HUT...

HE LOOKED UP AND SAW THAT THE DOOR TO THE HUT WAS STILL OPEN...

...BUT JUST A FEW METRES AWAY FROM THE HUT, LIONEL MISSED HIS STEP, TRIPPED AND FELL FLAT ON HIS FACE...

AT THE SAME TIME THE LION LEAPT IN AN ATTEMPT TO CATCH ITS PREY...

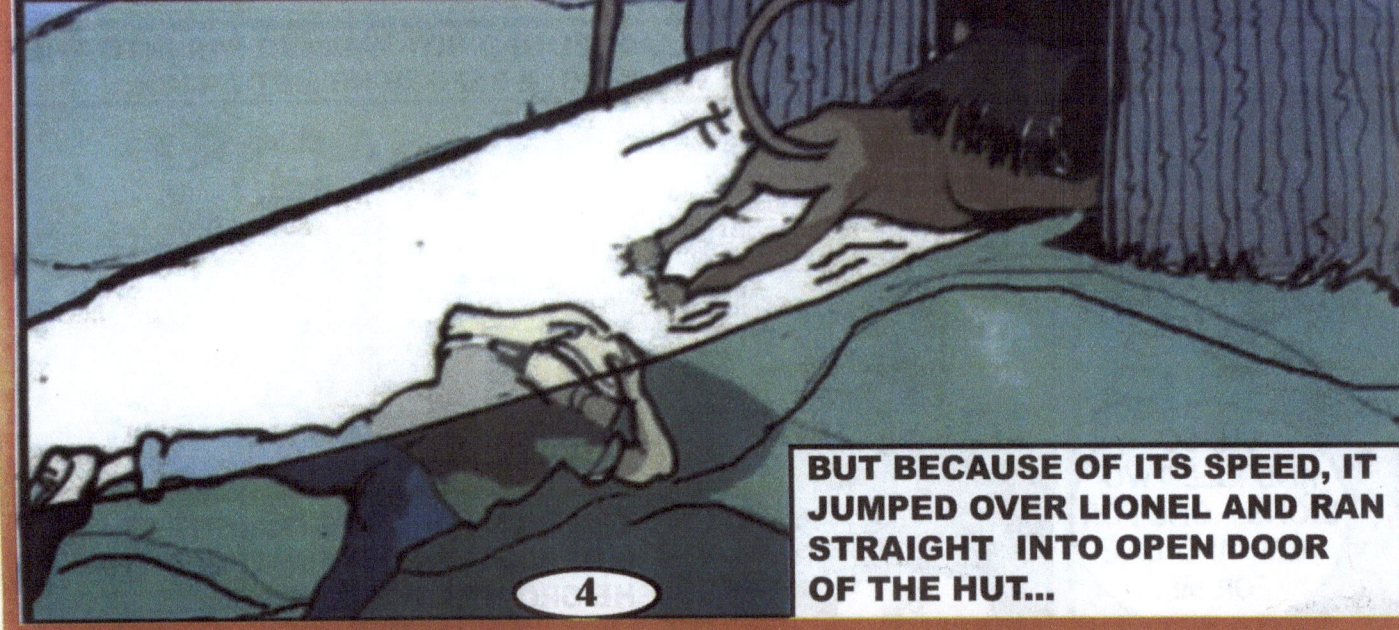

BUT BECAUSE OF ITS SPEED, IT JUMPED OVER LIONEL AND RAN STRAIGHT INTO OPEN DOOR OF THE HUT...

4

HIS HEART BEGAN TO BEAT FASTER, WITH SWEAT COVERING HIS FACE AND PALMS...LOOKING DOWN THE HIGH TREE, HE SAW HIS GUN LYING AMONG THE SHRUBS. THEN HE THOUGHT TO HIMSELF...

THANK GOD MY GUN IS STILL INTACT...

HM...I HAVE TO ACT FAST BEFORE I END UP IN THE BELLY OF THESE WILD CATS. BUT I MUST BE SURE THAT THE LION IS SECURELY LOCKED UP.

HE WAITED FOR ONE MORE HOUR THEN QUIETLY DESCENDED AND GRABBED HIS GUN...

END

CHECKING TO KNOW IT WAS STILL LOADED, HE SLUNG THE GUN OVER HIS SHOULDER AND WENT IN THE TRAIL OF HIS FRIEND, LIONEL.

IN THE ANIMAL KINGDOM ONE BEAUTIFUL MORNING, A MOTHER HYENA RAN INTO A LUCK OF A DEAD ASS.
THERE WAS MEAT ENOUGH FOR 3 WHOLE DAYS. SO SHE BEGAN TO ENJOY HER UN-EXPECTED MEAL.
GOOD NEWS
THEN SHE SUDDENLY LOOKED BACK AND SAW HER CHILDREN COMING. BUT BECAUSE SHE DID NOT WANT TO SHARE HER MEAL, SHE MISLED THEM...
HEY KIDS, THERE'S A LOT OF DEAD ASSES IN THE NEXT VILLAGE. GO QUICKLY AND GET YOURS'.
! ?
THE EXCITED YOUNG HYENAS RACED TOWARDS THE VILLAGE, SPREADING THE GOOD NEWS ON THEIR WAY...
1

AS THE NEWS TRAVELLED TO ALL CORNERS OF THE FOREST, OTHER STARVING ANIMALS CREPT OUT OF THEIR HIDING PLACES AND RAN AFTER THEM...

ALL MORNING, THE MOTHER HYENA WATCHED THEM RUSH BY...IN TENS AND TWENTIES...

UNTIL SHE STARTED TO BELIEVE THE STORY HERSELF. THEN OFF SHE WENT THINKING...

I MUST GO AND GET MY SHARE OF THE ASSES TOO

BUT ON GETTING TO THE VILLAGE, THERE WAS NO DEAD ASS ANYWHERE...

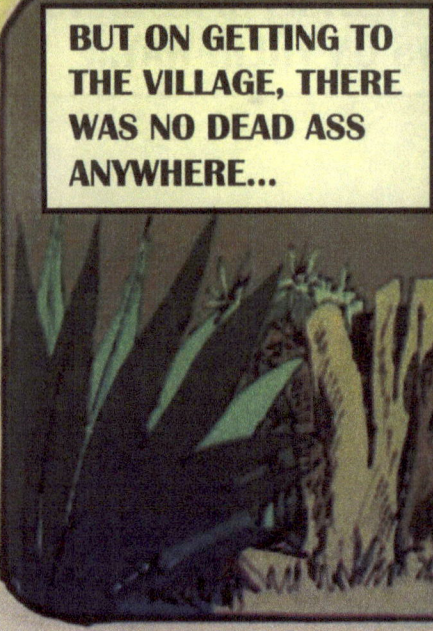

BAH! THIS PLACE IS EMPTY. NOT A SINGLE ASS

WELL, LET ME GO BACK AND FINISH MY MEAL.

3

AGAIN, SHE WAS DISAPPOINTED AS SHE MET OTHER ANIMALS EATING THE DEAD ASS SHE LEFT BEHIND.

?!

AND THE FOOLISH HYENA WATCHED HUNGRILY AND HELPLESSLY!

3

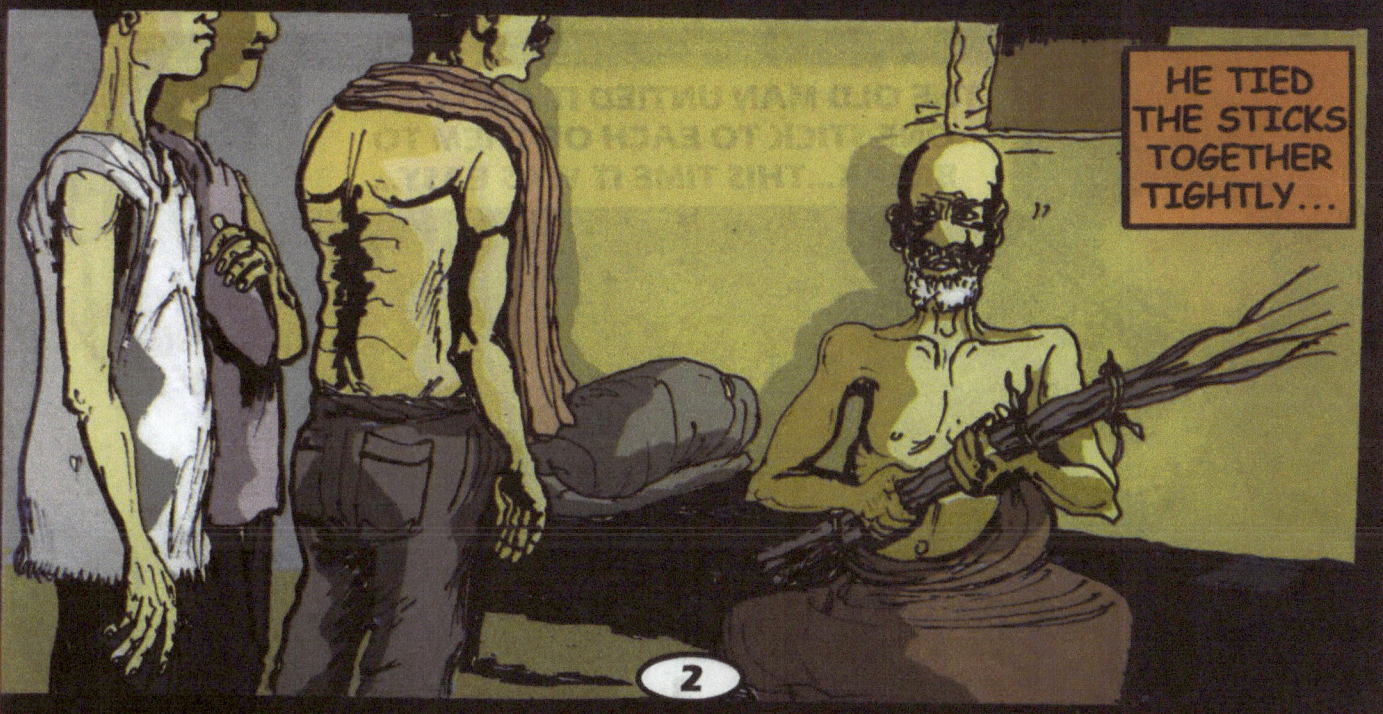

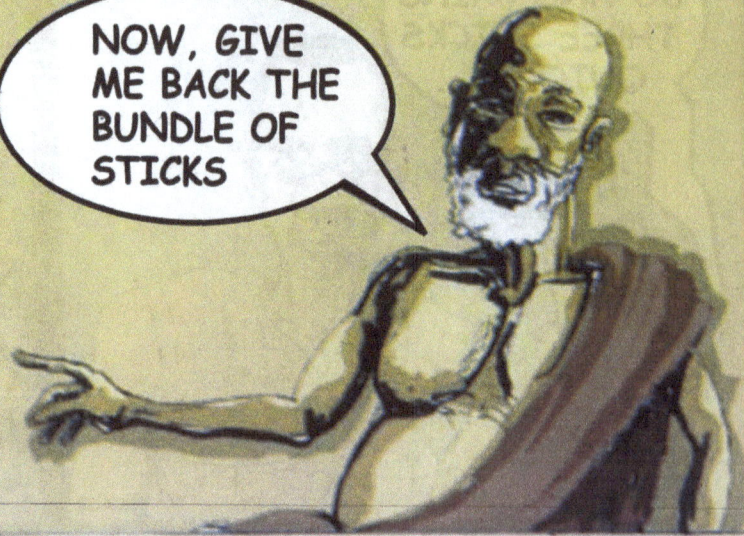

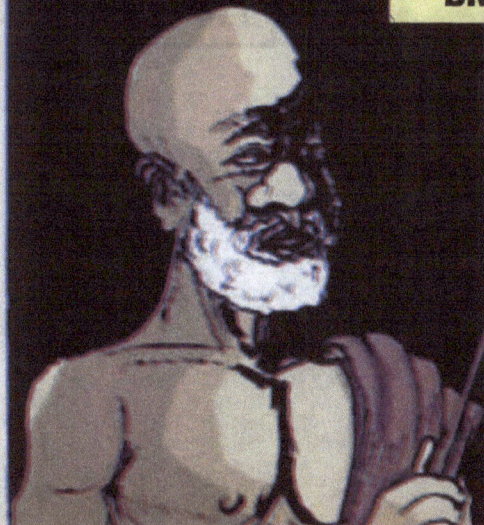

THE FIRST SON DID IT...

SNAP!

THEN THE SECOND

TWAK!

AND THE LAST

SNAP!

YOU MUST LEARN TO ALWAYS BE TOGETHER. IT WAS EAST TO BREAK THE STICKS BECAUSE THEY WERE SEPERATED. UNITY IS STRENGTH!

THEY ALL THANKED THEIR FATHER AND EMBRACED THEMSELVES AND VOWED NEVER TO QUARREL OR GET INTO ARGUMENTS AGAIN.

THE END

...CLOSE TO YOUR PLANTATION IS A BIG APPLE TREE...
YOU'LL SEE A BIG BLACK STONE
...ROLL IT AWAY AND DIG A HOLE... ONE SQUARE METRE AND TWO METRES DEEP. REPORT TO ME WHEN YOU FINISH
THE SERVANT COMPLAINED, BITTERLY AT THE NEW ASSIGNMENT THE KING GAVE TO HIM
AT THE END OF THE SECOND DAY, THE LAZY SERVANT DUG A HOLE OF ONLY ONE METRE DEEP
ONLY GOD KNOWS WHAT HE NEEDS A HOLE FOR
AND THE KING WAS SO ANNOYED WHEN HE CAME TO INSPECT IT
IS THIS WHAT YOU DUG, LAZY MAN.?

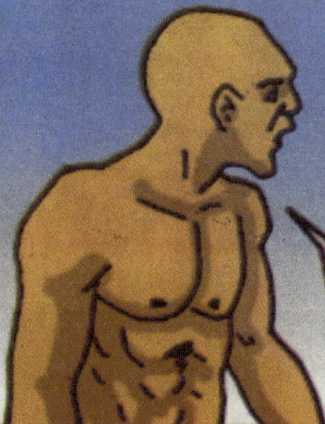

MEANWHILE, LINTU TOOK LINDA TO A HUT HE BUILT ON TOP OF A HIGH MOUNTAIN AT THE OUTSHIRT OF TOWN.

INSIDE THE HUT, HE PLACED LINDA ON TOP OF A BAMBOO BED HE HAD PREPARED. HE MOVED BACK, LOOKED AT HER AND WENT INTO ANOTHER SMALL ROOM...

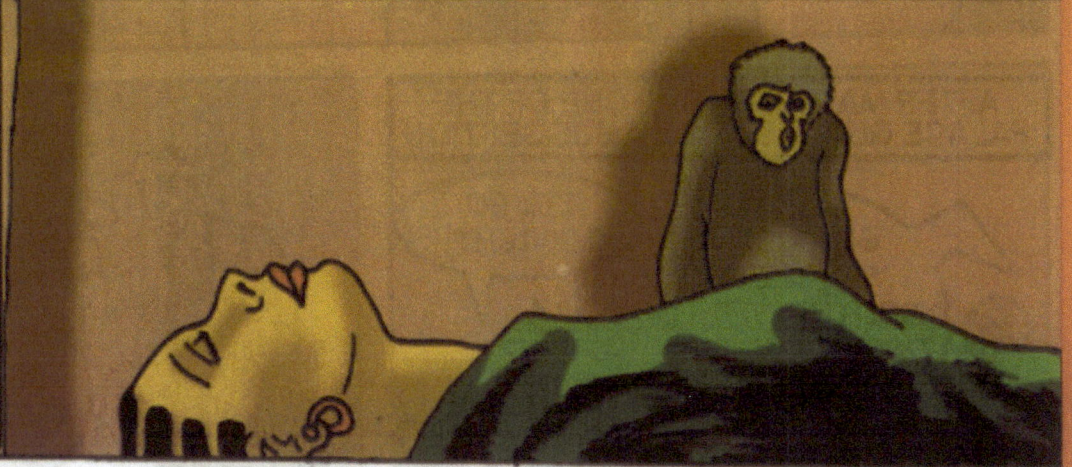

HE REAPPEARED IN HIS HUMAN FORM AND UNDID THE SPELL ON HER.

EMI OMO ALAPA TOROPA -TOROPA!

UGH!... MY HEAD... WHERE AM I?

THEN, SHE BECAME CONSCIOUS...

GOSH! IT'S LINTU THE WICKED MAGICIAN. WHAT AM I DOING HERE?

SHE CAN'T ESCAPE. THE MOUNTAIN IS HIGH AND SHE' ALWAYS IN CHAINS.

THIS MUST BE A DREAM. NO, IT'S NOT A DREAM

5

BACK IN BAMUDA, A LOT OF FUNNY STORIES ARE FLYING AROUND TOWN

SOME SAID SHE FLEW AWAY.

THEY SAY THE GROUND SWALLOWED HER UP!

OTHERS SAY SHE'S A WATER SPIRIT!

AFTER MANY MONTHS, ONE OF THE PALACE GUARDS MADE A SUGGESTION

GO AND SEE THE SOOTHSAYER IN THE OTHER TOWN MY LORD!

I'LL GO TONIGHT.

WELCOME YOUR HIGH-NESS...

AT MID-NIGHT, THE KING SET OUT ON HIS JOURNEY.

I MUST GET TO THE ROOT OF IT.

HE ARRIVED SAFELY.

WELCOME YOUR HIGH-NESS...

I'M TROUBLED JAMBITO, MY DAUGHTER JUST VANISHED INTO THIN AIR!

JAMBITO WENT INTO HIS INNER CHAMBER.

WAIT YOUR HIGHNESS

6

...AND RIGHT BEFORE THEIR EYES, THE VULTURE TRANSFORMED TO A HUMAN BEING...
IT'S LINTU THE WICKED MAGICIAN!
AFTER SEVERAL ATTEMPTS, ONE OF THEM CLIMBED TO THE TOP OF THE HILL
HELLO LINDA, ARE YOU SAFE?
LINDA WAS RESCUED AND BROUGHT TO THE KING. SHE LOOKED SO EMACIATED DUE TO LACK OF CARE FROM LINTU.
WELCOME HOME DAUGHTER. I MISSED YOU SO MUCH.
I MISSED YOU TOO DAD!
THAT NIGHT, THE KING THREW A BIG PARTY. THERE WAS A LOT TO EAT AND DRINK AND EVERYONE WAS HAPPY BECAUSE LINDA WAS FINALLY BACK.
ALL STORIES TO BE CONTINUE IN VOLUME 2

ADVERTISE ON THE NEW KIDZMAG - ITS YOUR BEST DECISION OF A LIFETIME

www.ingramcontent.com/pod-product-compliance
Lightning Source LLC
Chambersburg PA
CBHW042001100426
42813CB00019B/2947